A culinary tour of Poland proves to be full of surprises, for the wealth and diversity of Polish cuisine is encountered in every one of the country's regions. Traditional breads and cold meats, preserves home-made from fruit and vegetables, excellent honeys, and a range of dishes made from grits and potatoes not to be met with anywhere else. And to top all those off, another Polish speciality – one or other of the exquisite fruit liqueurs.

So all that it remains for us to do is to wish you a very sincere Bon Appétit!

Polish Cooking

Polish Cooking

text
Izabella Byszewska

photography
Christian Parma

 Wydawnictwo PARMA® PRESS

Introduction
You are invited to the table...

*A*nd the table is a well-filled one, for laid out on it are all the best things that the pantries and storehouses of the "Commonwealth of Many Nations" can come up with. For, for several centuries now, traditional Polish cuisine has really been a mosaic of Polish, Lithuanian, Byelorussian, German, Jewish, Ukrainian and Tartar delicacies – one put in place through years of co-existence within a single state. And to be added to that are the distinct tastes of such Polish regions as Silesia, the Podhale, the Podkarpacie (Subcarpathians), Kashubia, Kurpie, the Podlasie and Wielkopolska (literally Great Poland), as well as the interwoven recipes from what could be afforded by the peasantry, the nobility and the gentry, the class of self-made magnates, and – from the 19th century on – the mercantile middle classes as well. It is from such sources that our menu has acquired the *paysanne* delights of *żurek* soup, and the more "lordly" pleasures of almond soup, beautifully prepared zander or crayfish, the Silesian *krupniok* version of the Polish black pudding or *kaszanka*, the Lithuanian sausage known as *kindziuk*, the Tartar *pierekaczewnik* (a filled roulade of layered pastry), the potato pate from the Podlasie known as *babka* and the Jewish Chulent.

The Polish larder has long been augmented by diverse ingredients from further afield – ever since the days of the eastern wars, or the northerly excursions made by overseas merchants into Poland via the "Moravian Gate". This is how *bakalie* (dried fruit and nuts) came to be with us, as well as Hungarian wines, a wide variety of exotic herbs and spices such as the beloved saffron, and... the gingerbread that Toruń is so famous for, but also the Lower Silesia, and Biecz in the Podkarpacie. It was not only new products that came to enrich Poland's cuisine – there were also hitherto-unknown methods of preparing dishes and of processing foods. The traditional fried cheese of Wielkopolska is a delicacy invented by Silesians above all, as well as Germans inhabiting western Poland. Also deriving from German cultural circles are such favourites in Cieszyn-Silesia as the *zozworki* ginger biscuits (*zozwor* being the Silesian word for ginger), as well as the typically Silesian cold meats like *salceson* and *wątrobianka* liver-sausage (otherwise *preswurst* and *leberwurst*). It is in turn to our eastern neighbours that we owe the *kiszki* and potato *babka* prepared in the Lublin or Podlasie regions, as well as smoked fat-bacon and the different *pierogi*, plus the various steamed dumplings known as *pampuchy* or *parowańce*. Then there are the cakes for different religious ceremonies – led off by the yeast cake *korowaj*. Polish culinary traditions are still cultivated very solicitously, especially by the inhabitants of regions of strong cultural identity, like Kashubia region extending south-east from Puck and Gdańsk

on the coast as far as Chojnice; the Podhale region in the Tatra Mountain foothills; the various Beskid ranges in the south west; the forested Kurpie region north of Ostrołęka; the Wielkopolska region around Poznań; and the border regions within which Polish influences intermingle with those of neighbour countries. Nor should we forgot the mix of influences arising in Silesia, Pomerania and the Mazury region – formerly German-influenced areas into which Poles from the Eastern Lands lost after World War Two were resettled. It is everywhere possible to encounter clear linkage with the cooking habits of old – these having been transferred in recipes, or best of all by demonstration, from one generation to the next. So such quaint old words and dishes as *mamałyga* (a sweet-corn bake) survive to this day, having been brought to Poland by highlanders from the region of Bukowina. Likewise, Poles from Lvov (today's Ukrainian L'viv) brought with them the art of making *kandybał* – a honey-and-lemon drink, while Silesians specialise in the fruit dessert *szpajza*, as well as in *zymlok* – a kind of forcemeat. Each region on Poland's culinary has its own foods, these relating not only to local culture, but also to the more fundamental climatic and geographical conditions. Thus the menu in Kashubia runs to a plethora of fish dishes, but also includes items based around goose and duck. And – since the soils here are poor – much has had to be accomplished with the rutabaga and pumpkin – vegetables that can tolerate such conditions. The Kurpie lands were similarly impoverished, but what the area lacks in terms of *charcuterie*, it makes up for in dishes based around cabbage, potatoes, and honey from the area's extensive forests. The real paradises for lovers of cold meats and sausages are in turn Wielkopolska, Kujawy (Cuiavia), the eastern part of Mazowsze (Mazovia) and the hill and mountain region of the south known as Małopolska (Little Poland). For almost 200 years now, these regions have been working to perfect their smoked and pickled hams, juniper sausage, smoked goose, various lards, black puddings, *salceson* sausages and streaky bacons... For that matter, there is no way to miss out the Podhale with its sheep's cheeses, notably *oscypek* (a hard smoked version), *bryndza* (a soft cheese), *bundz* and *redykołka*. Dishes from buckwheat grits are what the Lublin region (particularly the Biłgoraj area) are famous for, while the Podkarpacie boasts dishes based on cereals and hulled millet. Sandomierz is the place for orchard fruits, while the Podlasie has its *sękacz* – a spit-roasted layer cake made of eggy mixture. So, if all that seems in any way tempting, let us invite you without further ado on a culinary tour around the pantries of Poland!

Breakfast
For a good start to the day

*A*s in the mid 19th century, so also today, many people prefer to start their day with a coffee and cream. And while it is true that we no longer hold to the tradition espoused by one chronicler a hundred years ago – to the effect that what matters at breakfast is that it be "fatty, sweet and in large amounts", and while we do not expose our empty stomachs to the delights of a slug of aniseed- or cumin-flavoured vodka followed up by a roasted plum, we 21st-century folk do still cultivate a remarkable number of "oldy-worldy" customs when it comes to food. If we were to try and define the products and dishes identifying today's typical Polish breakfast, we would surely put bread first – and very probably we would mean one of the sourish leavened rye breads so typically Polish. On top of that we would doubtless seek to mention some cured or smoked cold meat, and most especially one of those ever-so-many different kinds of Polish sausage. Add to that fine jams, in particular a nice plum jam from the Lower Vistula Valley, Małopolska or the Podkarpacie, and then honey or a cottage cheese of soured cow's milk – maybe with herbs or vegetables. A particularly well-renowned example of the latter might be Wielkopolska's *gzik*. But then of course there are the aforesaid sheep's cheeses from the mountain foothills, for example *bryndza* or *oscypek*. As recently as in the mid 20th century, things were done differently in town and country. The typical rustic breakfast had to feature something hot – perhaps noodles or potatoes or grits with milk, sometimes a *żurek* soup, and then in later years also scrambled eggs, or fried eggs on fat bacon, or streaky bacon or sausage, even with tomatoes and onions on the side. Traditionally, that lot would have been washed down by a grain coffee with milk, though cocoa went with yeast cake on a Sunday. Manor-houses would in turn have served wholemeal bread or rolls home-baked, along with home-cured cold cuts, home-made jams and honey and – in particular where a hunt was anticipated – hot dishes like *bigos* made with cooked sauerkraut, devilled kidneys, smoked goose, red beet soup, or broth... Just over a decade ago it was still pretty much obligatory for Poles to take "milk soup" at breakfast, this featuring one or other kind of kasza (probably barley or wheat) cooked in it, or else a pasta or sweetened egg and flour mixture. Today, we rather find bread and butter, cold meat and cheese, as well as honey and jams, eggs (especially soft-boiled or scrambled) and vegetables in season (mainly tomatoes and cucumber). The rhythm to which the Polish larder was stocked resembled so much else here in having religious connotations. Unsurprisingly then, a visitor's fullest insight into Polish cuisine will have to wait until Christmas or Easter. At these times in particular, the serving of certain dishes and products seems "obligatory". Poles even paid attention to the preparation of foods suitable for fast-times, notably Good Friday as such, or Lent in general. Such dishes emerging in the "light" version frequently utilised legumes, potatoes and grits of various kinds, along with oil, onions and – more often than not – pickled herring. To this day, a country market stall should be able to supply the special kind of oil required, which even goes by the name of "holiday oil" in some regions. In fact, this is oil pressed cold, by traditional methods, from flax, rape or linseed. The "full" version of fast-time food is in turn seen best in regions with plenty of lakes and rivers, since people living there see fit to consume a variety of freshwater fish, including pike, carp, tench and zander. Lent is preceded by the lengthy "Carnival", during which the appetite can be endlessly and variously satisfied. Today's version of Carnival cuisine seems virtually as speciality-filled as it ever did, a key element being cakes, notably Polish-style doughnuts (traditionally filled with rose jam), as well as those long, brittle and distinctly fat-rich strips of sweetcrust pastry known as *faworki*. Easter-Day breakfast assumes feast-like dimensions, the table groaning under cold meats and sausages, with smoked or boiled ham taking pride of place. Alongside that there might be slices of roast pork fillet served cold, bacon, and roasted white sausage. Silesians would tuck into meatloaf, while residents of the central Mazowsze region might favour a stuffed pig. The unique *żurek* soup referred to already is a characteristic Easter dish, it being a member of the group of white borsch soups with a deliciously sour taste. It is based around rye flour, though the additions vary from region to region, be they small cubes of cold meat, hard-boiled egg, white sausage or horseradish. As a rule the cakes will include *babki* – as dome-shaped yeast-cakes with raisins, nuts, etc. added; the decorative shortbread-like *mazurki* topped off with dried fruits, nuts and icing; and of course cheesecake. Painted or hand-coloured boiled eggs are also sure to be present, as are sugar or butter lambs recalling Christ as the Lamb of God.

Morning delicacies

Honey

This inseparable companion of the Polish breakfast is used in the same way as jam, to top the meal off on a sweet accent. Poland has long been famous for its honey, with almost every region boasting its own flower types giving honeys of specific types and tastes. Particularly prized are the honeys made from fir-tree nectar around Nowy Sącz, as well as the buckwheat-flavoured honeys from the Lublin region and the Podkarpacie, the heather honeys of Lower Silesia and Pomerania, the lime and multi-flower varieties of the Kurpie and Warmia-Mazury and the kinds made from *Phacelia* in Wielkopolska. Yet there are also even rarer specialist kinds, such as those made by bees visiting raspberry or bean flowers, meadow flowers in general, or hawthorn.

Butter

Until just a couple of decades every country housewife made her own butter out of cream from the farm or smallholding's own cow(s). Today, however, such natural butters are a rarity. What remains common is the modification of purchased butter into various kinds of flavoured varieties. Crayfish butter was once one of the most refined elements of Polish cuisine, being prepared with mashed boiled crayfish necks. Garlic butter is a perennial favourite, as are types seasoned with chives, dill or various other herbs.

Cheeses

Poland's most famous cheese is undoubtedly the Highlanders' smoked sheep's cheese known as *oscypek*, as well as a whole range of other varieties made from sheep's milk in the Podhale region, i.e. *bryndza*, *bundz* and *redykołka*. Central and Eastern Poland form the realm of the cottage cheeses, while residents of Wielkopolska could not imagine breakfast without *gzik* – a cream cheese served with onion or chives, or else a fried cream cheese concoction with cumin seeds. Also renowned are the rennet cheeses of the Podlasie and Suwalki regions, as well as those made from the milk of a growing number of farm goats.

Morning delicacies

Eggs

Offered in various guises, eggs are typical ingredients of a Polish breakfast. Ever-popular are the soft-boiled egg or eggs scrambled on butter, additional ingredients being streaky bacon, ham, onion or tomato. A delicacy of the mushroom-picking season is provided by scrambled eggs with chanterelles, and omelettes served with jam or vegetables have many fans. Further favourites are hard-boiled eggs garnished with mayonnaise or filled with a mushroom or fish paste.

Jams

The best of the thinner, runnier, jams is probably that made from the *Węgierki* plum variety, with no extra sugar and with subsequent "baking" in a bread oven. The Vistula Valley and the Podkarpacie regions have specialised in this product, and they still support large orchards of the plums in question. And housewives keep up with the traditional recipe. More generally, pretty much every Polish pantry had to have its jam prepared with large amounts of sugar. Those made from cherries, strawberries, raspberries or apricots were held in the highest regard, and jam remains an inseparable feature of the Polish breakfast. Favourites are perhaps the tarter blackcurrant or redcurrant jams, or else those made with gooseberries or apples. It is also quite common for jams to be made from mixed fruit.

Bread

Foreigners are just amazed by the diversity of Polish bread, though the king surely remains the traditional rye loaf made with natural leavening and without any improvers or preservatives. Beyond that are the various wheat- and/or rye-flour wholemeal or white breads. Where prolonged freshness is an issue, "additives" like boiled potato or semolina have little to do with chemistry. Herbs and the seeds of sunflowers, pumpkin or flax may also all go in, or on, our bread, which is still baked in a brick oven, on horseradish or cabbage leaves. Also standard at breakfast are bread rolls, along with sweet *chałka*, butter rolls and the bagel-like *obwarzanki*.

Gzik

Wielkopolska

3l fresh unpasteurised milk,
2 tablespoons home-curdled milk,
cup cream,
large onion or spring onion,
salt and pepper

Add the sour milk to the fresh milk, and put aside in a warm place until all has become sour. Then heat the milk over a low flame until it curdles. Squeeze the whey through a linen cheesecloth, before pressing the mass under a weighted board. Mix the cheese obtained with cream, adding finely-chopped onion or spring onion and salt and pepper to taste. The gzik can be served with jacket potatoes as a lunch.

Fried cheese with cumin

1 kg of soft cream cheese,
$^1/_3$ packet butter,
2 egg-yolks,
1 tablespoon cumin

Grind the cheese down finely in a bowl, mixing in the cumin towards the end of the process. Cover the mixture with a linen cloth and leave in a warm place for 2-3 days. When fermentation begins, melt the butter on a pan and fry the cheese on a low flame, mixing frequently to ensure a uniform mass is obtained. Add salt to taste. While still hot, mix in the raw egg-yolks thoroughly. Then transfer the mixture to a bowl and refrigerate. Serve as a spread for bread.

Gomółki with herbs

Podkarpacie

1 kg white cheese,
4 egg-yolks,
salt,
selected herbs (especially finely-
-chopped mint, fennel/dill,
parsley, basil and/or thyme)

Mix the cheese and egg-yolks together thoroughly, adding the herbs at your discretion. Form walnut-sized balls from the mixture and place in the oven to dry slowly at moderate heat.

Lard with apples

Warmia-Mazury

1 kg fatback,
100 g streaky bacon,
onion,
3 cloves garlic,
2 tart apples,
teaspoon marjoram,
salt and pepper

Cut the bacon and pork fat into cubes, melt, then cool down and mince. To the fat add very finely diced apple and onion, as well as crushed garlic. Fry gently, add salt, pepper and the marjoram, and then combine with the pork crackling. While heating, mix well before pouring into earthenware pots or jars.

Kindziuk

Podlasie

A pig's stomach,
1 kg choice cuts (ham,
shoulder or fillet of pork),
40 g salt,
1 g saltpetre ,
milled pepper,
allspice,
1 clove garlic

Wash the stomach thoroughly, scrubbing as necessary, then scald with boiling water before rinsing again in cold water. Cut the meat into small pieces, before adding the saltpetre and spices, and leave for several hours. Then, pack the meat very tightly into the stomach so that no empty crevice is left, before sewing up with cotton and hanging in a cool place to dry. After several days, smoke in a cool smoke from the branches and leaves of broadleaved trees, adding juniper branches every so often for the sake of the scent. *Kindziuk* should be smoked for periods of 2-3 hours over several days. The larger the piece, the longer the period of smoking.

Mixed meat paté

Wielkopolska

500 g pork (e.g. shoulder, ham),
120 g raw fatback,
250 g calf's or pig's liver,
500 g beef,
100 g stock-vegetables,
60 g stale roll,
3 eggs,
juniper berries,
1 bayleaf,
allspice,
nutmeg,
salt and pepper

Boil the meat with the vegetables and bayleaf for 1½ hours, adding salt half way through the cooking process. Towards the end put in the fatback (leave several slices for the baking) and cook for 25 minutes more. Remove the membranes from the liver, cut up, then pour out 1²/₃ cups of stock and simmer the liver in it for 5 minutes. Soak bread roll in 30 ml of the stock. Squeeze the meat and liver, add the bread, allspice and juniper. Pass the whole mass through a mincer twice, using a fine mesh the second time. Add salt and grated nutmeg, pepper and the eggs, and mix well. Place the slices of fatback at the bottom of a baking tin, which is then filled three-quarters full with the paté mixture. Brush the top over with egg white and place in a pre-heated oven. Bake for about 1 hour at 200°C, until the sides of the paté are brown. Serve with horseradish.

Pumpkin racuszki

Podlasie

250 g pumpkin,
cup curdled milk,
cup flour,
2 eggs,
tablespoon oil,
oil for frying,
salt

Mix the milk, egg-yolks and flour in a bowl with coarsely-grated peeled pumpkin. Add salt, oil and beaten egg-whites, mixing gently.
Heat the fat on a frying pan, spooning on to it a not-too-thick layer of mixture which is then fried slowly until golden-brown.
Serve the *racuszki* with sprinkled sugar, cream or jam.

Plum jam

Kujawy-Pomerania

3 kg of węgierki plums
(picked late and slightly wrinkled)

Boil the plums in a large, flat pan, then simmer for several hours over a low flame. Stir regularly to avoid burning. When just around $^1/_3$ of the original volume remains, steam off. Press through a sieve into a basin, place in a medium oven (at c. 140ºC) for further slow evaporation, until the jam runs off the spoon, and a "skin" forms on the surface. Transfer to jars and pasteurise.

Easter Breakfast
Stuffed eggs

Łódź region

24 eggs

Fish filling:
8 yolks of hard-boiled eggs,
smoked herring, or a tin of sprats
or anchovies,
salt and pepper

Ham filling:
8 yolks of hard-boiled eggs,
100 g ham,
1 teaspoon mustard,
salt and pepper,
paprika

Mushroom filling:
8 yolks of hard-boiled eggs,
a few dried wild mushrooms,
1 tablespoon of cream,
salt and pepper.

Hard-boil the egg, remove the shell, cut into half lengthwise and remove the yolk. Prepare fillings in line with the instructions below, then spoon into the depressions in the egg-whites.

Fish filling: Mash up the egg-yolks with the fish until a smooth mass is obtained, then season to taste.
Ham filling: Mash up the egg-yolks with finely chopped ham and mustard, seasoning with salt and pepper.
Mushroom filling: wash the wild mushrooms, soak in water for half an hour, then cook in the same water. Drain off, put through a mincer together with the boiled yolks, then mix in cream, salt and pepper.

Easter ham in pastry

Podlasie

1½ kg ham,
horseradish leaves,
2 teaspoons each of marjoram,
thyme and summer savory,
2 cloves garlic,
salt and pepper

For the pastry:
2 cups graham or wholemeal flour,
4 eggs,
20 g yeast,
1 cup milk,
1 pinch salt

Press the crushed garlic into the ham before wrapping in horseradish leaves and soaking for 24 hours in salted water to which half of the herbs have been added. Then remove, prick, and rub in the remaining herbs and pepper. Make the dough, knead, leave to rise, then wrap around the ham. Bake in the oven for around 2 hours at a temperature of 150-170 ºC.

Traditional żurek

Podkarpacie

For the essence:
500 g wholemeal
(rye or oat) flour,
crusts of wholemeal bread,
3 cloves garlic,
1 litre warm pre-boiled water

For the soup:
Stock-vegetables,
250 g bacon or ribs,
bayleaf,
4 fairly large potatoes,
½ teaspoon marjoram,
cold meat (sausage,
bacon, ham),
100 g of each,
2 tablespoons
fresh grated
horseradish,
2 tablespoons cream,
salt and pepper

Essence: Tip the flour and breadcrusts into a stoneware basin, slowly pouring in the water so that a liquid mixture is obtained.
Add a crushed clove of garlic. Leave the basin in a warm place. Next day, pour off the excess water, add a similar amount
of fresh pre-boiled water (cooled) and the other 2 (crushed) cloves of garlic. The liquid essence will be ready after 3 more days.
Easter żurek: Prepare 2 l of stock from the stock-vegetables plus bacon or ribs, adding the bayleaf also. Add potatoes cut into strips
and cook until the latter are soft. Slowly pour in the well-mixed essence, mixing steadily. Cook, season with salt, pepper and marjoram.
The żurek should be thick. Add diced cold meats, fresh horseradish, two tablespoons of cream mixed with flour and cook further.
Serve with eighths of hard-boiled egg.

For the cake mixture:
5 eggs,
100 g sugar,
150 g flour,
1 heaped teaspoon
baking powder

For the butter-cream:
2 packets butter,
200 g icing sugar,
1 packet vanilla sugar,
vanilla-flavoured *budyń* (blancmange
– like powdered dessert),
500 ml milk,
50 ml rectified spirit,
1 tablespoon orange liqueur

For the decoration:
500 g marzipan,
½ bar plain (bitter) chocolate,
almond flakes,
chopped hazelnuts,
raisins

Grind the egg-yolks and sugar together into a paste, steadily adding sifted flour to which the baking powder has been added. Mix,
add the whisked egg-whites and stir gently once again. Pour the sponge-cake mixture into a greased rectangular-shaped baking tray or dish.
Preheat the oven to 170° C. Bake for 45 minutes, cool and cut into two sheets. Prepare the *budyń* from hot and then leave to cool.
Cream the butter in firmly with the icing sugar, adding the vanilla sugar and then – mixing firmly and constantly – the *budyń* and the spirit.
Sprinkle the liqueur across the cake sheets and then spread on the butter-cream in between them. Heat the marzipan in a pan
with the chocolate, before spreading across the surface of the *mazurek* and decorating with fruit and nuts.

Babka yeast cake

Wielkopolska

500 g cake flour,
80 g yeast,
cup milk,
8 egg-yolks,
200 g sugar,
packet vanilla sugar,
200 g butter,
half teaspoon salt,
100 g raisins,
3 tablespoons rum

Pour boiling milk on to half of the flour and mix thoroughly to a paste. Add finely-chopped yeast, mix in and leave the mixture to rise. Grind together the sugar, vanilla sugar and egg-yolks until a fluffy mass is obtained, then combine the mixture with the risen dough, adding in the remaining flour and salt and making the dough ready. Melt the butter and pour in, along with the rum, before mixing until a smooth consistency is obtained and the dough no longer sticks to the fingers. Finally add the raisins (first washed and then dried) and mix them in, before placing the dough in a greased savrin-type pudding mould and leaving to rise. Once it has risen, brush the surface of the babka with egg white and bake for about 1 hour at 180ºC.

Roasted white sausage

Łódź region

1 kg white sausage,
4 small onions,
fat for roasting,
horseradish

Roll the sausage up into a wreath. Melt fat in a shallow pan and place the sausage in it. Peel the onion, cut in half and lay around the sausage. Place in a well-heated oven and bake at a temperature of 200ºC until the surface of the sausage browns. Serve on a dish with the onion, garnished with horseradish.

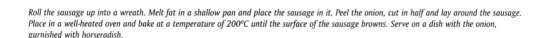

The abundance of the afternoon

Lunch

It is more or less to the 18th century that the routine regarding mealtimes can be traced. Breakfast was mostly eaten between 8.00 and 9.00, a small (or not-so-small) snack at around 11.00 known as second breakfast, lunch between midday and 16.00, and then tea or supper between six and eight in the evening. Like many other countries, Poland had its dishes fit for everyday consumption, and those whose appearance denoted Sundays and feast days. No matter where in society one might be, there was more in terms of both quantity and quality on a Sunday. The meat or poultry was better (or present at all), the bread and the cakes of white flour. This remains true today, notwithstanding changes in civilisation and mentality. Indeed, the foods eaten and times at which they are taken are little different now from how they once were.

The meal Poles still consider most important is lunch. This always had an integrating function where family and guests were concerned. Even today, when the coordination of family lunchtimes in the working week may prove impossible, most of us still sit down to a shared lunch on Sundays and at various holidays. In this way, the traditional soup, main course and dessert have managed to come through from the distant past to the present day.

While the traditional Polish luncheon has really changed quite a lot down the centuries, one might be surprised just how many dishes served back then are still put on the table today. As in the 17th or 18th centuries, so also today we consume noodles for lunch, along with buckwheat patties and various kinds of grits. Chicken broth and red beet soup are classical dishes coming through to the present in largely unchanged form, and the same could be said for meat with horseradish. Likewise, a diary account written 200 years ago described luncheon at Duke Karol Radziwiłł's residence in Nieśwież, mentioning "tripe with ginger, duck with capers, turkey with almond sauce", and later "carp browned with honey", as well as less well-known fish like vendace and ruffe. Equally, the feast featured certain dishes now known only from literature, like nose of moose, bear's paw, and boar's head in spicy sauce...

The Polish lunch resembles other meals in drawing from regional tradition still cultivated in many households, especially on Sundays and holidays. Thus the typical Sunday lunch in Wielkopolska is polewka, i.e. a whey- or buttermilk-based soup, followed by steamed yeasty noodles accompanying roast pork in sauce, or stuffed roast duck. Red cabbage has to be there, while dessert most often takes the form of an apple strudel or makocz – a yeast cake with poppyseeds. In Silesia they serve żurek – a white borsch, as well as beef roulade or a meatloaf accompanied by Silesian kluski, and szpajza – a kind of lemon mousse – for dessert. The most popular soups in Mazowsze, produced on high days and holidays, are chicken broth, and the red beetroot borsch known in Poland as barszcz. There might also be potatoes, hard-boiled eggs or beans. The typical main course might be beef with horseradish sauce, roast pork with cabbage, beef olives or beef stews and goulashes. These are served with potatoes, boiled, mashed or baked, as well as buckwheat. Fruit compote is the likely dessert, or else a cake or the kind of set jelly- or blancmange-like desert known as kisiel, which contains potato flour. Eastern parts excel in the production of flour- or potato-based dishes, most especially the famous pierogi, often equated to ravioli, in as much as they are envelopes stuffed with meat, white cheese, cabbage and mushrooms, or different kinds of grits. The various sweet pierogi are in turn served with bilberries, raspberries, plums or cottage cheese. Podlasie boasts the potato babka and kiszka, while the Lublin area has its buckwheat pierogi and kulebiak – a flat yeast dough mainly filled with meat and mushrooms.

The role of compote may not be underestimated – a watery drink from boiled fruit mostly served with the pieces left in. For many, a lunch without it is hard to imagine, just as in the past.

Polish culinary tradition has created specific menus for Christmas Day and Easter Day. Goose, turkey or roast ham were customarily consumed to celebrate the former, while the latter festivities saw Polish village folk turn, not to hot meals, but to a rich array of meats with such condiments as horseradish sauce, ćwikła (mashed boiled beetroot, often also with horseradish), and various marinated and pickled fruits and vegetables. Of course, that lot could only be eaten with rye bread and bread rolls, all with yeast cake to follow.

Lunches frugal and festive

Dumplings, a Polish answer to ravioli and pancakes

Classic lunch items are a list of flour-based products headed up by the ravioli-esque *pierogi*, which may be boiled, baked or fried and are variously filled with buckwheat or millet grits, commonly with white cheese, or often with lentils, minced beef or pork, or even offal. Christmas Eve suppers across Poland feature *pierogi* with cabbage and wild mushrooms, but others are served sweet, with fruits of the forest – as may be the various steamed *kluski*, "noodles" if long and narrow, but also served up as the more substantial potato-based *pyzy* or *knedle*, or the *pampuchy* "boiled buns", spherical in shape and containing both wheat flour and yeast. Yet another kind of meat-stuffed potato dumpling is known (via a perceived resemblance to munitions) as *kartacze* ("grape-shot"), *kanony* or *bomby*. Pancakes with sweetened white cheese or jam are also popular dessert.

Noodles

A classic main course in Silesia comprises beef roulade served with round, flattened noodles with a depression in the centre and red cabbage, or else the "iron" noodles made from grated potato. Home made chicken or beef broth is always served with handmade macaroni noodles, or else the drop-noodles formed as egg-flour mixture is tipped into the boiling soup. With *kopytka* we are back with the less noodle-like noodles, these being made from a flour and mashed potato mixture, often served with roast beef. In turn, the second course in Wielkopolska is often served with *rwańce* – torn-off pieces of a dough made with flour, milk, butter and yeast cast into boiling water; while the *kładzione kluski* served in Mazowsze are steamed items made from flour, butter and eggs of longer shape (the name meaning "laid down").

Compotes

The home-boiled compotes were traditionally the housewife's pride and joy. From June onwards, the pantries of Poland became steadily filled with compotes put aside for the winter, having been boiled up from ripe strawberries, raspberries, gooseberries, currants, bilberries or apricots. These were joined in autumn by apple, pear or plum compotes, sometimes even accompanied by freshly-cracked walnuts. Even today, a lunch is often taken with compote to drink, or as a separate fruity dessert. Compotes can of course be mixed to improve the effect, and may be further sweetened through the addition of a light syrup made from peaches, pears or white plums. A particular kind of addition to other deserts is a compote made from such old-fashioned pear varieties as *bergamotki*, these having been boiled into a thicker syrup with added lemon juice, cinnamon and cloves. Old Polish cuisine also made use of the "sharp" compotes, wherein wine vinegar was added. Particular favourite fruits for this treatment were pears, plums, sour cherries, melon or pumpkin, these offering an excellent complement to roasts or cold meats.

Lunches frugal and festive

Salads

The classic side dishes accompanying a main course were the "Polish salad" or Polish *mizeria*, i.e. sliced cucumber in cream with sugar, served with roast chicken above all. This all goes down best when served cool on a hot summer's day, perhaps with lemon juice and fennel as well. The same kind of sauce may go on crisp green lettuce, often with quarters of boiled egg. Another classic *crudité de la maison* in season is the well-known tomato salad served with diced onion or chives. The winter salad of greatest importance (from the nutritional as well as cultural points of view) was and remains a concoction of white- or red-cabbage sauerkraut – a vegetable traditionally present in every Polish home from the peasant's cottage up to the lord's castle. Apple, onion or carrot goes in alongside the cabbage, the dressing being of cumin seeds and vinegar, or lemon juice plus oil. Leek salad with cream is another traditional possibility, while another typical *crudité* comprises grated celeriac and apple served with cream or mayonnaise.

Lunches frugal and festive

Vegetables

It is impossible to imagine a roast on a Polish table without the classic accompaniment of boiled and mashed beetroot, often served with finely chopped onion fried in butter, thickened with flour or else served with soured cream. White-cabbage sauerkraut raw or cooked goes just fine with roast pork or pork escalopes, served without or without onion; while the fermented cabbage expands into a full fast-day meal if cooked up with peas, beans or dried mushrooms. Boiled red cabbage or *modra* is a favourite in western Poland and Silesia, this going along with roast fowl –particularly goose or duck, or else beef. Another popular vegetable mixture in Poland comprises boiled and diced carrot served with peas and served sweet. Cauliflower is also boiled, the taste being enhanced by the scattering over it of butter-fried breadcrumbs.

Sauces

Meat served cold is accompanied by a range of cold sauces – a kind of tartar sauce involves the fine-chopping of eggs, with the addition thereto of pickled cucumbers, while there is also a horseradish sauce with oil and cream (with honey as a further optional ingredient). Mustard or fennel sauces complete the lineup, along with the various salad dressings based around oil, vinegar, mustard and garlic. An exquisite addition to meat is provided by cranberries and cowberries, served raw with sugar, or boiled up into preserves, with or without added pear and apple. *Ćwikła* is a fine addition to cold meats, made of grated beetroot and horseradish. No self-respecting Easter breakfast is complete without it. The hot sauces of old Poland traditionally accompanying meat dishes were in turn the beer sauce, onion sauce or "white" sauce with lemon, the "grey" sauce with which the Christmas Eve carp was served, horseradish sauce, fruit sauces, and a wide range of mushroom sauces.

Kapuśniak – cabbage soup

Małopolska

1½ litres water,
500 g sauerkraut,
5 large potatoes,
smoked rib,
500 ml soured cream,
onion,
tablespoon lard,
teaspoon cumin,
salt,
bayleaf,
pepper

Cook the rib until it is almost soft, add the cabbage, pepper, bayleaf and cook on, until the cabbage also softens. Remove the rib, strip off the meat and cut into pieces. Cook the potatoes, then crush them in the water in which they cooked and combine with the cabbage mixture, adding in the diced meat. Heat the lard and lightly fry in it the cumin and onion (chopped finely), adding the product to the soup. Improve with cream to taste and serve with bread.

Black soup

Lubusz Land

goose off-cuts
(offal, wings, neck, etc.),
1 litre water,
stock-vegetables,
100 g prunes,
50 g dried apples,
goose blood,
2 tablespoons flour,
allspice,
1 bayleaf

Boil up a broth from the stock-vegetables and meat, adding the dried fruit towards the end. Remove the offal from the broth, mix the blood with flour and add to the stock, then boil on, returning the offal to the soup in finely chopped form. Serve with noodles or mashed potato.

Traditional broth

Mazowsze

1 whole chicken,
250 g turkey breast,
200 g veal,
2 large carrots,
4 small parsley roots,
2 medium-sized onions,
bunch parsley,
bunch dill or fennel,
salt,
coarse-ground pepper,
allspice

Place the chopped-up chicken, turkey and other meat in a large pan of cold water, along with the carrots (scraped). Cook, skimming off as necessary and adding the parsley root (scraped) and the onions, as well as the bunches of parsley and dill. Add salt, cook on a very low flame, removing any scum that forms. When the parsley root is soft, add a tablespoonful of fresh butter, as well as several peppercorns and allspice berries. Cook on for around 15 minutes. The total cooking time for the broth should not exceed 2 hours. Serve the soup with noodles (preferably home-made), sprinkling parsley on the surface.

Country-style thick pea soup

300 g dried peas,
400 g mixed pork cuts (shoulder,
ham, off the rib),
100 g streaky bacon,
100 g pearl barley,
1 carrot,
1 parsley root,
1 onion,
5 medium-sized potatoes,
salt,
marjoram

Sort and wash the peas before soaking overnight in pre-boiled water. Parboil the next day, leave in the water for two hours, then strain through a fine sieve or liquidise. Cook the pearl barley with the meat until soft, then add the diced stock-vegetables and potatoes, boiling on until the latter are soft. Add the strained pea mass and mix in. Cut up the bacon, fry with onion and add this to the soup as well, seasoning with salt and marjoram. Chopped parsley may be scattered on the soup as a finishing touch.

Traditional cold soup (chłodnik)

Mazowsze

1½ litres curdled milk or kefir,
500 ml cream (18%),
1 bunch radishes,
1 bunch chives,
1 bunch dill,
1 bunch parsley,
1 bunch young beetroot stems,
1 large cucumber,
2 cloves garlic,
¼ cup beetroot concentrate,
1 tablespoon sugar,
salt and pepper,
1 tablespoon lemon juice

Chop the beetroot stems up finely, cooking up in a small amount of salted water, then cool. Add the curdled milk or kefir (having first whipped it up), plus the cream and beetroot concentrate and mix. Cut the chives up finely, likewise the parsley and dill, then dice the cucumber and radishes. Add all to the soup. Add in mashed garlic, salt, sugar, pepper to taste and the lemon juice. Mix gently, then place in the fridge for several hours. Serve with hard-boiled eggs.

Gołąbki

Lublin region

medium-sized cabbage
with soft leaves,
250 g minced pork,
250 g minced meat
from breast of young duck,
cup rice,
large onion,
egg,
3 teaspoons cream,
2 tablespoons tomato
concentrate,
1½ tablespoons flour,
salt and pepper,
allspice,
bayleaf

Sear the cabbage leaves with boiling water, and cut off any coarser parts. Save the water used. Mix the meat thoroughly with the onion (finely-chopped), the egg, salt and pepper. Boil rice so that it remains separate, add to the meat and again stir the mixture thoroughly. The filling obtained in this way should be placed on the cabbage leaves, which are then rolled up tightly around it. Place the gołąbki so formed in a deep pan, cover with several cabbage leaves and pour in the water left over from the scalding process. Add the bayleaf and several berries of allspice, and cook under cover until the cabbage is soft. The gołąbki may also be baked in the oven, in an oven-proof dish. To the stock in which the gołąbki have cooked, add a sauce made from the flour, cream and tomato concentrate plus a few tablespoonsful of water. Cook on, adding salt and pepper. Gołąbki can be served with potatoes or bread.

Kartacze

Podlasie

3 kg potatoes,
300 g pork,
200 g beef,
150 g streaky bacon,
2 onions,
clove garlic,
pepper and salt,
tablespoon fat

Mince the meat, then add the garlic (crushed) and the onion (diced and lightly fried in fat). Season to taste with salt and pepper, and mix. Peel the potatoes and rewash them before grating on a tray, and squeeze out the juice into a bowl for starch. Add the latter to the mixture, which should be seared with boiling water and worked into a flexible dough. Form the meat mixture into balls and wrap these in dough such that an oval shape is conferred. Put into boiling salted water in a pan large enough to allow the *kartacze* to float freely. Cook on a low flame for around 1½ hours, then drain off. Serve with a topping of fried streaky bacon and part-fried onion.

Potato pancakes

Podkarpacie

5 large potatoes,
3 eggs,
200 g stale roll,
milk,
½ cup cream,
40 g yeast,
1 teaspoon sugar,
oil for frying,
salt

Soak the roll in milk. Peel the potatoes and grate finely, squeezing out excess water. Remove the bread, break up into small pieces and mix with the potatoes. Add the yeast, cream, egg-yolks and sugar, and salt to taste. Mix thoroughly and put aside to rise in a warm place. When the mass has risen, combine it with the whisked egg-whites, mix gently and fry thinnish pancakes until brown on both sides. Serve with fresh or soured cream or with a mushroom sauce.

Bigos

Świętokrzyskie region

1½ kg fresh cabbage,
1 kg sauerkraut,
300 g pork (shoulder, picnic shoulder),
300 g roasting beef,
200 g smoked streaky bacon,
200 g good roast sausage,
150 g cold meats (ham, *baleron*, bacon, sliced loin),
500 g lard,
50 g dried wild mushrooms,
150 g destoned prunes,
2 onions,
1 glass dry red wine,
salt and pepper,
1 bayleaf,
several berries dried juniper and allspice

Cut the fresh cabbage up into thin strips and scald these with boiling water. Add water, the bayleaf and the allspice, as well as the onion (this having first been chopped finely and fried in hot fat until clear), and cook the mixture until the cabbage is soft. Squeeze out the sauerkraut, add the wild mushrooms (parboiled and sliced), juniper and prunes and pour in the stock from the mushrooms. Cook on a low flame until the cabbage softens. Add the parboiled fresh cabbage and three cups of water. Dice the pork, fry in lard and add with the fat to the cabbage. Cook on for around 3 hours on a low flame, taking care to ensure that burning does not take place. Set aside until the next day and then cook on for a further 3 hours, before once again setting aside for several hours. The beef, bacon, sausage and other meats should be cut up and fried lightly in lard before being added to the bigos. Cook for a further 2-3 hours, until the cabbage assumes a golden brown colour. Half an hour before serving, add the wine, and salt and pepper to taste, and simmer on for 10-20 minutes.

Necówka

1 kg minced pork (shoulder,
streaky bacon, stewing pork),
500 g beef tenderloin,
2 onions,
5 egg-yolks,
2 cloves garlic,
marjoram,
cumin,
salt and pepper

Mix the minced meat with the egg-yolks, herbs and spices, stirring well and creating a cylindrical shape, in the centre of which the salted
and peppered tenderloin is inserted. Seal up in aluminium foil and roast for about 1 hour in the oven at 180ºC. Cool and then place in the fridge.
Serve sliced for eating with bread, or reheated as a main course.

Roast turkey with juniper

Mazowsze

1 turkey (3½-4 kg),
80 g butter,
2 onions,
2 cloves garlic,
10-20 dried juniper berries,
salt and pepper

Clean the turkey and peel back the skin from the legs in order to remove the hard tendons. Then, by cutting the skin along the back, separate the meat and skin from the bones, leaving the legs and upper parts of the wings. Rub salt over the meat prepared in this way, along with pepper and the juniper berries crushed. Set aside for 12 hours. Tie up the legs, then rub butter over the meat, place on a baking sheet covered in aluminium foil or in a baking tray and put in a very hot oven and roast at 220°C until brown. Turn over, basting with several tablespoonfuls of water, lowering the temperature and roasting for around 1½ hours, continuing to baste with the gravy produced by the bird and checking for tenderness with a fork. Serve the turkey with roast potatoes or chips (French fries), along with cowberries or cranberries or a sweet pickle, or else with red cabbage.

Duck with cranberries

Pomerania

duck with giblets,
300 g minced pork,
2 tart apples,
100 g prunes,
egg,
onion,
marjoram,
basil,
garlic,
pepper and salt

Rub the herbs and spices on to the inner and outer surfaces of the deboned duck, and refrigerate for the night. Next day, chop up the giblets (offal) and mix with the minced meat, adding the egg and seasoning to taste. Stuff the duck, adding pieces of apple and prunes, though holding some back for the sauce. Heat an oven to 180° C, put the duck in a baking tin and roast for around 40 minutes, basting with water. Add the remaining apple and prunes and roast for a further 30 minutes, continuing to baste with the gravy being produced. Serve with fried potatoes and cranberry sauce.

Roast boar

Lubusz Land

2½ kg raw boar ham,
½ cup double cream,
flour,
allspice,
juniper berries,
1 bayleaf,
salt and pepper

For the marinade:
1 litre water,
½ cup vinegar,
2-3 bayleaves,
allspice,
crushed juniper berries,
2 crushed cloves of garlic,
½ teaspoon each of cinnamon,
marjoram, coriander, tarragon
and thyme,
¼ teaspoon each of pepper
and cumin,
several cloves,
100 g onions

Boil up the water with the vinegar, bayleaf, allspice, juniper, marjoram and salt, before leaving to cool. Rub thyme, coriander, tarragon, marjoram and garlic into the meat. Place in an earthenware basin, lay on slices of onion, and pour in the marinade in such a way that the meat is completely covered, add the cinnamon and some cloves. Set aside in a cool place for 5-6 days, turning the piece of meat several times. Remove the meat and rinse, then rub salt and pepper on to it and set aside for 1-2 hours in a cool place. Fry the ham lightly on all sides in a heated fat, then place in a baking tin and into a pre-heated oven. Baste with vegetable stock during cooking, at a temperature of 200°C. When the meat is tender, remove it, drain off the sauce and augment it with cream, cooking on for a short while over a low flame. Serve sliced on a dish, with millet grits plus fruit and nuts. Serve the gravy separately in a jug or sauce boat.

Roast lamb

Małopolska

1 kg leg of lamb,
onion,
2 cloves garlic,
juice of ½ lemon,
several berries of allspice,
bayleaf,
salt and pepper,
marjoram,
4 tablespoons oil

Rub all surfaces of the piece of meat with the herbs mixed with the crushed garlic and lemon juice. Place into a bowl with onion slices laid on the surface, cover and refrigerate for several hours. Remove from the fridge, reserve the herbs and onion and rub the meat with salt before browning on all sides on a high flame. Place in a pan with the oil, add the previously set-aside herbs and onion, soak with hot water and then cook until the meat is tender. Carve shortly in advance of serving, arranging the slices on a heated plate and surrounding with baked potatoes. Serve gravy separately, this being augmented if desired with 2 tablespoonfuls of yoghurt mixed with a teaspoonful of flour.

Crayfish necks

Warmia-Mazury

c. 30 crayfish or cooked
crayfish necks,
2 parsley roots,
1 bunch dill,
salt,
3 tablespoons cream,
200 g butter,
2 onions,
2 large cloves garlic

Cook the crayfish with the parsley roots, dill, salt and garlic. Remove the necks. Melt butter in a large frying pan,
frying up chopped onion and crushed garlic before adding the crayfish necks and frying them on all sides.
Then add cream and chopped dill for an excellent hot bite.

Cod in saffron

Western Pomerania

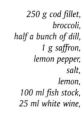

250 g cod fillet,
broccoli,
half a bunch of dill,
1 g saffron,
lemon pepper,
salt,
lemon,
100 ml fish stock,
25 ml white wine,

Marinade the fish in lemon, salt, lemon pepper and dill before frying. Sear the broccoli with boiling water
and with added salt and sugar. Prepare the sauce by adding the saffron and finely-chopped dill
to the heated stock. Add wine and browned flour and butter for a thicker consistency.

Oven-baked trout with garlic

Lower Silesia

4 trout,
2 tablespoons butter,
2 cloves garlic,
salt and pepper

Clean and gut the fish, salt the exterior slightly and sprinkle the inside with salt, pepper and crushed garlic.
In a baking tin melt half the butter and lay out the trout. Place a knob of butter on each and cook for about 30 minutes.
Serve with boiled water and a coleslaw.

Boiled beef Polish-style

Mazowsze

1 kg young beef off the bone
(rump joint or brisket),
stock-vegetables
plus savoy cabbage,
onion,
several peppercorns
and fruits of allspice,
1 quarter teaspoon cumin,
2-3 dried wild mushrooms,
salt

Horseradish sauce:
2 cups sour cream,
3 tablespoons grated
horseradish,
3 egg-yolks,
tablespoon butter,
tablespoon vinegar,
salt

Put the meat into around 2 litres of boiling salted water and cook for 30 minutes before adding seasonings, the stock-vegetables and lightly-fried onion still in its outer skin. Cook on a very low flame until the meat is tender. When cooked, slice across the grain to give well-formed escalopes, laying these out on a warmed plate. Cut up the vegetables from the broth, transfer to a pan, pour in the stock, add flour and salt and simmer for a while. Lay out around the meat on the serving dish, spoon on some horseradish sauce and scatter with dried breadcrumbs.

Prepare the horseradish sauce by mixing the cream with grated horseradish and the egg-yolks. Salt the mixture obtained and cook with a tablespoon of butter. Mix in vinegar when cool.

Ruthenian dumplings

Lublin region

For the mixture:
450 g flour,
2 eggs,
2 tablespoons oil,
warm water

For the filling:
1½ kg cooked potatoes,
1 kg cream cheese,
2 eggs,
150 g butter,
large onion,
2 tablespoons dried mint,
salt and pepper

Crackling:
150 g streaky bacon
or fatback,
large onion

Filling: Mince up the potato with the cream cheese and butter. Add the eggs, the onion (fried in oil until clear), the mint and seasonings. Mix in well.

Mixture: Sieve the flour onto a pastry-board, and knead in one egg, the oil and hot water so that the dough is not too heavy. Knead the dough very thoroughly, so that it no longer sticks to the board. Form the pierogi from circles or squares of the dough, add the filling and seal. Cook in a large amount of salted water to which a tablespoon of oil has been added. Fry small pieces of the fatback or streaky bacon with chopped onion and scatter over the dumplings.

Forest mushrooms in cream

1 kg fresh forest mushrooms
(various boletuses
or honey mushrooms),
2 tablespoons butter,
2 medium-sized onions,
tablespoon flour,
cup sour cream,
salt and pepper

Clean, wash and slice the wild mushrooms (preferably young). Peel and chop the onion and fry lightly in butter, not browning.
Add the mushrooms plus salt, and cook on a low flame under cover, mixing from time to time to prevent sticking.
When the mushrooms are soft, add flour, cook for a short time longer, then pour in cream, simmering on for a little while.
Season with pepper. Serve with potatoes sprinkled with dill or wholemeal bread with fresh butter.

Honey mushrooms

Warmia-Mazury

1 kg fresh edible boletus
mushrooms (small),
cup vinegar (10%),
3 cups water,
8 tablespoon multi-flower
or lime honey,
200 g small onions,
cloves,
white mustard,
4 teaspoons salt

Wash the mushrooms, cutting off the thicker lower stalks, leaving only the caps with a short tail. Place in boiling salty water
to which 1 tablespoonful of vinegar has been added and boil for 15 minutes, before draining and washing with cold pre-boiled water.
After drying, lay loosely in twist-top jars, adding 6 cloves and 10+ seeds of white mustard to each jar. To prepare the pickling mixture,
boil water with the vinegar, plus salt and the onions. Dissolve the honey in the still-hot (not boiling) liquid. Fill the jars with the liquid
in such a way that 2-3 onions end up in each. Put on the lids, before pasteurising for 15 minutes.

Ribs

Wielkopolska

350 g ribs,
50 g chanterelle mushrooms,
80 ml cream (36%),
50 ml red wine,
1½ tablespoons honey,
parsley,
rosemary,
thyme,
2 cloves garlic,
1 onion,
salt,
pepper,
oil

Prepare the marinade from the wine, honey, oil, rosemary, thyme and garlic, then stand the ribs in it for 24 hours, before oven-roasting under cover at 180° C. After one hour pour over the wine and roast on for another 15 minutes. Chop the onion finely and fry with the chanterelles. Add cream and simmer for a while until slight thickening takes place. Season with salt and pepper, finally sprinkling with finely-chopped parsley. The ribs in sauce may be served with Silesian potato noodles (*kluski śląskie*) and fried cabbage.

Beef olives

Silesia

800 g side of beef (top round),
100 g smoked streaky bacon,
150 g sausage,
1 soured cucumber,
2 onions,
several juniper berries,
several dried wild mushrooms,
1 tablespoon tomato concentrate,
1½ tablespoons flour,
3 teaspoons cream,
2-3 tablespoons oil,
salt and pepper

Cut the meat across the grain into escalopes and hammer until thin. Lay a rasher of streaky bacon along each piece of meat,
as well as a piece of cucumber sliced lengthwise. Roll up tightly, keeping the olives in place with thick cotton thread or cocktail sticks.
Then salt the olives, add pepper and roll in flour. Heat fat in a pan, cook the beef olives until brown, then add the wild mushrooms
(pre-soaked), the onions (sliced), the juniper berries and the sausage (chopped finely). Take a pan one-third filled with water and simmer
over a low flame until the meat is soft. Towards the end of the cooking, add a teaspoonful of flour, the cream
and the tomato concentrate to the sauce.

Soured cucumbers

1 kg medium-sized pickling
cucumbers (not fully ripe),
750 ml water,
1½ tablespoons salt,
several cloves garlic,
fresh horseradish root,
1 bunch dill with flowerheads,
several bayleaves,
several blackcurrant
or cherry leaves,
1 teaspoon mustard seed

Tightly pack the thoroughly cleaned and washed cucumbers vertically into washed and steam-sterilised jars. Each jar should receive a clove of garlic, a piece of horseradish, 1 bayleaf, several mustard seeds, a sprig of dill and a blackcurrant or cherry leaf. Boil water with the salt, and pour into the jars while still hot, in such a way that all the cucumbers are fully covered. Close the jars and leave at room temperature for 2-3 days, before transferring to a cool cellar or pantry.

Stew with tripe (flaki)

Mazowsze

500 g pork or veal tripe,
1 carrot,
1 parsley root,
1 small celeriac,
1 leek,
1 onion,
1 tablespoon lard,
2 tablespoons flour,
4 tablespoons cream,
salt,
pepper,
marjoram,
nutmeg

Clean and carefully wash the tripe, rinsing it several times. Then place in boiling water, drain, add fresh hot water and the onion and cook until soft. Remove the tripe, dry off and slice thinly. Slice the vegetables and cook them in 1 litre of water, before adding the tripe and fried flour+fat thickening, and boiling. When cooked, add salt, pepper, marjoram and grated nutmeg. Stir in the cream. Serve hot, with fresh white or wholemeal bread.

Fillet of beef with fruit

Lublin region

250 g beef fillet,
2 potatoes,
1 handful forest fruits (cowberries,
blackberries, bilberries),
50 ml dry red wine,
2 cloves garlic,
2 sprigs fresh rosemary,
6 large leaves spinach,
5 leaves lettuce,
pepper

Prepare a marinade of the wine, garlic and rosemary and leave the beef in it for 48 hours before grilling the meat. Cut the potatoes into half-moon shapes and fry in a chip pan. Heat the wine in a small pan, adding the fruit, sugar and garlic. Then simmer until the wine evaporates entirely. Serve the fillet of beef with the fruit sauce created in this way, garnishing with the lettuce and spinach in a vinaigrette dressing.

Tea
A sweet bite

*T*ea is a now-rather-forgotten meal taken between lunch and supper. Yet as recently as in the mid 20th century, this was still a significant social event. The teas served in the houses of the rural nobility (in Victorian times in particular) linked up with typical rituals and menus. This was an occasion for polite chat in a refined atmosphere – to which guests were frequently invited. In summer, a meal of suitable size and character was to be enjoyed on the veranda or terrace, or right out in the garden on some green lawn at which guests could enjoy themselves around a laboriously set-up table. A surprising abundance and diversity of finger food might be on offer – special teatime delicacies like sausage rolls or the equivalent stuffed with minced game, chicken salad, different kinds of cheese, roulade, and even caviar or herring. The meats hot and cold were accompanied by marinated mushrooms, or pears, plums and apples preserved in vinegar. Home-made bread with country butter accompanied the cold meats, as did honey and jams. A very interesting combination – in rural households in particular – was fresh cucumber spread with honey, a culinary tradition memorable enough to have come down to us in many a novel or journal from former times. First and foremost, though, teatime was for the sweet-toothed, who could enjoy a wide range of cakes, biscuits and pastries, most especially tarts and French-style pastries, buttermilk rolls, often stuffed with fruit or white cheese, home-made ice cream, jellies and blancmanges, custards and sorbets. Fruits of the forest took their place alongside their garden-grown counterparts. In summer, strawberries, raspberries, bilberries or wild strawberries were served with whipped cream. Interestingly, such rich fare was not only washed down with tea, for milk, coffee, water, juices and compotes would also have been served. Or perhaps something stronger, in the form of home-brews based around vodka, or mead, and then wine or home-brewed beers in later times.

Even honey was not just honey, for – depending on the location of hives – it could be based around lime, robinia, buckwheat, conifer trees or simply "many flowers", each type having its own very distinctive taste and aroma. Likewise jams would have been made from sour or sweet cherries, strawberries, rose-petals and even ... green tomatoes, a delicacy considered Poland's answer to fig preserve. Cottage cheese was most likely augmented with chives, baby onions, herbs or fruit (as with Wielkopolska's *gzika*), but it was not the only possible cheese, as there were also French or Swiss-style ripened varieties, and then sheep's cheeses (especially in the Podhale), and the local cheese, whatever it might be, since pretty much each manor house made its own last century. Likewise, bread was not then something to be purchased, with virtually every (country or town) home in Poland getting down to the lengthy chore of breadmaking at regular intervals. The bread was mostly sour, based around leaven that might be nurtured in a home for several years. Wholemeal bread from rye flour was baked as a rule, the more refined wheat flour being a less common treat. Buns and brioches were produced, plus buttermilk crescents and a whole range of cakes and cream cakes, the latter often served with hot chocolate.

As time passed, the big country tea of old transformed into a rendezvous over a coffee or tea and some small cakes only. The appearance of a distinct middle class in the late 19th century coincided with a flowering of cafe society. So teatime became a moment for meeting out of the house, in cafes to which the whole family came along, on Sunday in particular. To draw such crowds, locales had to outdo one another in their tasteful decor, as well as (of course) the richness and diversity of what came on the plates. The most famous establishments built whole reputations around their exquisite sweets, be these cakes, biscuits, tarts, gateaux or ice creams, all arranged and served with a certain indefinable artistry.

However, the tide turned against the institution of teatime at the beginning of the last century. The authoress encouraging more modern tastes would tend to use her household management guide or cookbook to dismiss tea as simply unacceptable. Thus, for Karolina Nakwaska (as cited from *Kuchnia i stół w polskim dworze* by Waldemar Baraniewski), tea was "more of an opportunity to satisfy the glutton than to offer any real or healthy nourishment." The words seem to have hit home, for – in Poland at least – the modern-day tea is mainly a meal for children. Immersed in the rat race, today's hard-pressed adult has little chance to cultivate any of the rituals associated with afternoon tea.

Teas for any time of the year

Cakes with fruit

Summer evenings feature various cakes incorporating or served with fresh fruit. The season begins with sponge fingers plus strawberries, rhubarb, raspberries or currants. Then the time arrives for bilberry, apricot or peach tarts on a short-crust pastry base. As plums and apples come into season, they top off yeast cake, or those ever-popular Polish versions of apple charlotte. In winter, fresh fruit gives way to marmalades and jams – eaten as they are or used in a Christmas strudel. The "Carnival" period in the New Year is in turn a time of deep-fried, sugar-coated doughnuts – most traditionally filled with rose-petal jam, or else plum preserve.

Preserved and candied fruits

Tea and jam go so well together. In summer and autumn, housewives would devote hours to turning a shortlived superabundance of strawberries, raspberries, currants, apricots, cherries, plums and "fruits of the forest" (cowberries, cranberries, bilberries, even rowan and elderberries) into preserves. "Dry" jams were also made – from pears, cherries or plums fried in a pan with sugar; as well as honey-fried nuts. Fruit might also be turned into sorbets; as well as fruit "cheeses" and various marmalades.

Alcohol

A good home-made liqueur or vodka is prized more highly than the shop-bought equivalent – on condition that best-quality spirit is used, and care taken to ensure steeping of the fruit for just the right length of time. And – most important of all - the product is laid down for at least 6 months in a well-sealed bottle. Home-made vodkas sweet or bitter are still made, root vodkas, and fruity orange, cherry, lemon or plum kinds. Cake always went well with liqueurs, so these were duly made with chocolate, coffee, cherry, orange, raspberry, wild strawberry, rose hips or ... eggs (in the *ajerkoniak* advocaat). Meads are a Polish speciality, the ratio of water to honey determining if we have a 1.5:1 *półtorak*, a 2:1 *dwójniak*, a 3:1 *trójniak*, or a 4:1 *czwórniak*. Other popular home-brews are beers of juniper berries and a touch of honey, various light fruit (especially apple, cherry, raspberry, gooseberry or redcurrant) wines, and true wine made from the vine growing out there on the patio.

Fruit teas

It has always been common for afternoon tea to feature, not true tea, but a fruit tea, perhaps lemon, orange or rosehip. The cool of autumn or winter can best be kept at bay with a warming tea made from the fruit and leaves of raspberries. This encourages sweating when one has a cold, and at these times the popular lime-flower tea may also be employed. In turn, a tonic for all that ails one comes in the shape of "fruits of the forest" tea infused from raspberries, bilberries, cowberries, blackberries, hawthorn and rowan.

Milky drinks

Summer teatimes were the moment for refreshing milk or cream drinks. The most traditional of all drinks – on offer since time immemorial - are the curdled milks or buttermilks, whose place is often now taken by *kefir* or yoghurt. Children love shakes made of milk, *kefir* or sweetened cream, often accompanied by fresh fruits of the season, be these raspberries, strawberries, bilberries or apricots. Frozen fruit or fruit from compote offers a reasonably authentic substitute in wintertime.

Regional varieties of cake

Easter means *babka* – an iced yeast-cake with raisins, nuts, etc., while Christmas is for poppyseed cake and *piernik* – a ginger sponge. Silesian festivities never pass without *kołacze* cakes made with poppyseeds, white cheese and apples, while the Podlasie is the realm of the *sękacz* layer cake made with 60 eggs... Kraków bakers were the first to invent *obwarzanki* (i.e. bagels), while a wedding in the Podkarpacie boasts the decorative cheesecake known as *kołacz weselny*. Kurpie has its hard biscuits with honey and carrots (the "secret" ingredient), and there are also small figures known as *byski* or *nowelatko* baked for luck. The New Year to Shrove Tuesday "Carnival" equals doughnuts, as well as those sugar-dusted slips of fried pastry called *faworki*. In Poznań, they celebrate St. Martin's Day with a kind of croissant filled with white poppyseed mixture plus dried fruit and nuts. Finally, tea is taken with brittle biscuits home-pressed from a machine and including ... pork crackling.

Deep-fried doughnuts

Silesia

1 kg flour,
2 cups milk,
cup sugar,
packet butter,
60 g yeast,
10 eggs,
half a vanilla stick,
icing sugar,
rose or cherry jam,
¾ l oil for frying,
salt

Chop up the yeast with 3 tablespoons of warm milk and 1 tablespoonful of sugar, then put aside to rise. Sift the flour into a bowl, adding the leaven and the egg-yolks previously ground into a paste with the sugar and vanilla (chopped). Stir the mixture, pouring in warm milk and combining gently. Melt the butter and add to the mixture, before working further until a quite loose consistency is obtained. Put aside to rise until volume has doubled. Lay out the dough on a board and divide into equal-sized pieces slightly compressed. This amount of dough should be enough for around 50 doughnuts. Heat the rose jam, strain the cherry jam and insert into each doughnut, before resealing and leaving to rise. Heat the oil in a wide, thick-bottomed pan before testing heat with a single doughnut – if it floats the temperature is good for frying. Place the doughnuts in the fat and cover. When the doughnuts have turned reddish beneath, turn over and continue frying, now uncovered. When doughnuts are cooked evenly, remove, dab off excess oil and sprinkle with icing sugar. Place side by side to cool.

Deep-fried pastry twists (faworki)

500g flour,
5 egg-yolks,
3 tablespoons cream,
tablespoon spirit,
1 kg lard,
150 g icing sugar

As if making pasta, knead a dough comprising the flour, egg-yolks, cream, spirit and a pinch of salt. Roll out and reroll the dough for about 20 minutes, until bubbles appear. Divide the dough into parts, roll out very thinly and cut into strips about 3 cm wide and 15 cm long. Cut a 5-6 cm slit down the middle of each strip of pastry, push one end through the hole and pull to achieve the twisted shape.
Heat the lard in a saucepan or frying pan – the temperature is just right when a piece of pastry put in rises to the surface – and browns – rapidly. Fry the *faworki* on both sides until a pale golden colour is obtained, then dry off on paper towel.
Sprinkle with icing sugar when cool. Serve in pyramid formation on a cake plate.

Cheesecake with meringue topping

Małopolska

Mixture:
250 g butter,
3 cups flour,
3 egg-yolks,
½ cup sugar,
1½ teaspoons baking powder

The cheese mass:
1 kg smooth cream cheese,
1 cup sugar,
500 ml milk,
3 eggs, cream *budyń* (blancmage
like powdered dessert),
½ cup oil,
the juice of 1 lemon

Grind the sugar and egg yolks into the cream cheese, adding (in that order) the oil, *budyń*, lemon juice and milk. Knead the resultant mixture before applying to the base and sides of a baking tin. Then add the cheese mass. Bake for 40 minutes at a temperature of 170ºC, before beating the whites of the eggs, adding in the half-glass of sugar and spooning this over the surface of the cheesecake as a soft meringue topping. Bake on for around 20 more minutes.

White charlotte

600 g flour,
300 g butter,
150 g icing sugar,
1 teaspoon
baking powder,
3 egg-yolks,
2 tablespoons
soured cream,
3 tablespoons
dried breadcrumbs,
1½ kg tart apples
(e.g. of the *antonówka*
or *reneta* varieties),
1 quarter-teaspoon cinnamon

For the icing:
100 g sugar,
20 g butter,
3 tablespoons milk,
whipped cream for decoration

Sift the flour with the baking powder and icing sugar. Place on a board and chop in the butter, then add the egg-yolks and cream. Knead the resultant dough and refrigerate for 2 hours. When the dough has cooled, roll out into two large sheets. Place one layer on the base of a tin. Peel the apples and slice thinly, mixing in the cinnamon and breadcrumbs. Then lay the mixture evenly across the pastry dough, before covering with the other layer, sealing the edges and pricking the surface with a fork. Place in a hot preheated oven and bake at 180ºC until a skewer comes out free of mixture. Mix in the sugar with the milk and butter until the mixture becomes stiff and cover the cake with it. When cool, cut into rectangles and decorate each with whipped cream.

Silesian kołacz

For the cake dough:
750 g flour,
6 egg-yolks,
200 g butter,
50 g yeast,
1½ cups milk,
the grated rind of 1 lemon,
salt

For the poppyseed mass:
750 g poppyseeds,
400 g sugar,
250 g butter,
2 egg-whites,
tablespoon finely-chopped almonds,
tablespoon chopped walnuts,
3 tablespoons honey

For the crumble topping:
150 g flour,
80 g icing sugar,
80 g butter,

Pour boiling water over the seeds, soaking for several hours before drying, passing through a sieve and grinding thoroughly, adding the sugar. Mix with the whisked egg-whites, the fruit and nuts, the butter (melted) and honey.

Crumble topping: Chop up on a board the butter, sugar and flour. Cool greatly and then grate coarsely.

Dough: Prepare leaven from yeast plus 1 tablespoonful each of warm milk, sugar and flour, before setting aside. To the risen dough, add the flour (sifted), mixed with the sugar and egg-yolks first creamed together, plus warm milk, a pinch of salt and the lemon rind. Mix thoroughly into a good dough, before adding the melted fat gradually and mixing on until the dough again loses its shine. Leave for 30 minutes before halving the risen dough and rolling out. One layer (the base) should be 50% thicker than the other layer. Spread the base with the poppyseed mass, then cover with the top layer. Brush the surface with a mixture of 1 egg plus half a cup of warm milk, and scatter over the crumble topping. Bake in a medium oven for c. 40 minutes at a temperature of 170ºC.

Strawberry mousse

Świętokrzyskie region

500 g strawberries,
½ cup milk,
2 eggs,
2 tablespoons sugar,
¾ cup double cream,
1 teaspoon lemon juice,
2 teaspoons gelatine,
several walnuts

Separate the egg yolks and whites and bring the milk to the boil. Mix the egg-yolks with the sugar and mix in well with the milk, before beating until the mass becomes stiff. Add the strawberries (chopped), whipped cream and gelatine and cool.
Serve the mousse in small dishes, decorated with single specimen strawberries and walnuts.

Kashubian legumina

Pomerania

4 eggs,
2 lemons,
cup sugar,
packet gelatine,
double cream,
several slices of lemon
for decoration

Wash the eggs, separate the yolks from the whites, then beat the latter with a teaspoonful of sugar until stiff. Grind in the egg-yolks with
the remaining sugar in a bowl over steam, until a soft mass is obtained. Scald the lemons with boiling water then grate some rind
and squeeze the juice out into the yolk mixture. Suspend the gelatine in a quarter of a cup of cold water. Combine gently the egg-yolk mixture
with the beaten egg-whites and add in the gelatine. Put into small bowls, decorate with the double cream (whipped) and lemon slices,
and leave to stand in a cool place.

Sugar-fried pears

Wielkopolska

2 kg pears,
2 kg sugar,
3 cups water,
½ teaspoon citric acid

Boil up 1½ kg of the sugar with water, removing any scum. Peel the pears and halve, removing the core and pips. Steadily add the fruit to the boiling syrup, so they float freely. Cook on a low flame for about 5 minutes, then remove and set aside for several hours. Then reboil, adding citric acid to the syrup, and cooking on for 4-5 minutes. Skim and then set aside until the following day. Drain off the pears, adding the remaining sugar to the syrup. Then reheat, skim and return the pears to the syrup, stewing them in it for about 5 minutes until glazed. Leave until the following day, then reheat, carefully removing the fruit from the (very) hot syrup and placing them in steam-sterilised jars. Pour over leftover syrup in moderation and seal the jars tightly. Serve as a dessert in its own right or as a decorative element.

Bread drink

Podlasie

500 g rye bread,
500 g sugar,
200 g baker's yeast,
100 g raisins,
2 lemons,
10 litres water

Cut the bread, dry it out, then pour hot (pre-boiled) water on to it. When cool, add the yeast and sugar and set aside for 12 hours.
Then sieve and bottle, adding several raisins and one slice of lemon to each bottle and screwing on the tops tightly. Keep in a cool place.
The acid is ready for use after 24 hours.

Rowanberry liqueur

Podlasie

1 kg rowan berries,
2 litres strong spirit,
4½ cups sugar,
500 ml water

Pick the rowan berries after the first frosts, wash, destalk, etc., then dowse several times with boiling water. Tip into a demijohn and add 1 litre of strong spirit. Leave at room temperature. After two weeks, prepare a syrup from the sugar, water and the remainder of the spirit. Boil, skim, add the spirit drained off from the fruit and leave for 24 hours. Then strain through filter-paper into bottles.

Supper
An evening shared

In the old days, what was "on the menu" for supper differed little from what might be anticipated when people broke their fast at start of day. The żur(ek) soup with potatoes would reappear, as sometimes augmented with pork fat or bacon. All the different kinds of kasza would be there, or potatoes with soured milk. There were various potato dishes, in the east especially. These included the still-popular potato bakes and pates known as kartoflarze and babki. In the Lublin, Kielce and Łódź areas one could expect to be served prażucha, made from potatoes mashed with flour; while in the Podlasie there is the forcemeat with potato called kiszka ziemniaczana, as well as the pancake-like racuchy and flat griddle-cakes with baking soda. The gentry also ended the day with dishes served hot, though obviously with a more refined menu than could be expected in a peasant hut. Thus pork cutlets might come out of the kitchen, roast hare, fish dishes, crayfish or wild mushrooms in cream sauce. On top of that, hams, goose or various pates. A very important element of any traditional Polish supper were liqueur drinks home made by steeping dogberries, cherries or raspberries in vodka. The alternative might be meads, as well as straight vodkas or krupnik – a spirit served hot with spices and honey. To this day, one might use these to wash down a plate of cold meat, herrings or pigs' trotters in jelly. But today's supper Polish-style is primarily of cold meat, cheese, smoked fish, bread (rye and white), butter, vegetables and pickles (especially pickled mushrooms). We also still like our lard here, with onions, apples or mushrooms (each region has its favourite way of consuming spreadable pork fat), and definitely soured cucumbers or gherkins to complement all that. In general, the arrival of guests is equated with a need to bring out something hot – a stew of tripe or fish, the legendary bigos (cooked sauerkraut with meat and sausage), and different potato or rice bakes. The summer variant might in turn include soured milk with potatoes, all sprinkled over with bacon bits or pork crackling. The most important church holidays were always extremely important reference points when it came to the compiling of menus. The traditions that developed are very much upheld to this day. Christmas Eve is a time of "fasting" – in terms of types of food, if certainly not amounts. So cold or cooked meats and poultry are off the menu, while the number of dishes that are "on" varies from one place to another.

In Mazowsze, there can be various numbers of dishes, but the number must be odd, while in the Podlasie there are to be 12 dishes – one for each Apostle. Tradition also demands that an extra place be set for the unexpected guest who might arrive. And before supper begins, the hosts and guests break the thin Christmas wafer called opłatek together. Now as in the past this is made in monasteries. In many places, straw is placed under the snowy-white table cloth, to recall the manger in which the newborn Jesus lay. It also helps to secure good luck in the upcoming year, as well as good yields on the farm. Each Polish region has its Christmas Eve dishes. The kisiel served in the Podlasie is not quite like that elsewhere, this being an oatmeal dish with cold-pressed oil, sometimes with added milk plus poppyseeds and raisins, or honey. In turn, no pre-Yuletide spread in the eastern Podlasie, Podkarpacie or Lublin regions can do without kutia – a very ancient dish of poppyseed mass served with wheat or barley, honey and dried fruit and nuts. This meal also found its way into western Poland (mainly Lower Silesia and Western Pomerania) on account of the post-War resettlement here of people from eastern territories seized by the Soviet Union. Christmas Eve in Małopolska means moczka – a soup of drilled, dried plums, while Silesians bake zozworki ginger biscuits, and inhabitants of Mazowsze must have their dried-fruit compote. Soups are an important component no matter where one is, though from region to region the favourites might be red beet soup served with uszki (like small-scale pierogi) or beans – in Mazowsze; fish soup – in Pomerania and Kashubia; or soup of wild mushrooms – in Kujawy and the east of Poland in general. At the more refined end of the scale, Christmas Eve was marked by the appearance on the festive table of almond soup. Cabbage is pretty much always going to be there, though again its accompaniment might be wild mushrooms, peas or beans, depending on where we are. Likewise, the Christmas Eve pierogi might be with white cheese, or cabbage and mushrooms. Then last – but not least – there are the fish – in jelly, fried, baked or boiled with vegetables, and carp, zander or tench, to say nothing of the herring – in oil, in cream or pickled – served as an appetizer. Topping all that off are the cakes, also such traditional favourites as poppyseed cake, ginger cake, apple strudel, cheesecake and yeast-cake with dried fruit and nuts.

Suppers hot or cold

Condiments to go with meat

The taste of cold meats is much spiced up by a smaller or larger portion of horseradish, best of all newly-grated with a little sugar and lemon juice, or cream if the aim is to cool things down a bit. The Łódź area is famous for its horseradish, and specialists there have been engaged in the growing of one particular variety for more than 60 years now. Also very much prized is the boiled mashed beetroot known as *ćwikła*. What happens to that depends on where in Poland one finds oneself. In Mazowsze, it is in fact the aforementioned horseradish in cream that is added to confer a little tang upon the beets. In Pomerania, in contrast, the beetroots are sliced and served with apple, soured cucumbers, sugar and lemon juice. Boiled or fried sausage, frankfurters or bacon are complemented with traditional mustard from the jar, or else from freshly-ground green mustard cabbage. A spicy tomato ketchup has also been in use in Polish cuisine for more than 100 years now.

Cold meats

Each region has its own cold meats. Lower, Upper and Opole Silesia are home to some very popular German-style products: *presswurst* - otherwise *salceson*, *zymlok* – a pate-like affair, and *krupniok* blood sausage. They serve a ham on the bone called *soldra* in Małopolska, while cold smoke-cured *kumpia* can be expected in Kujawy and the Podlasie. The central Mazowsze region specialises in a dried "hand-stuffed" and "knife-sliced" sausage of unminced pork or pork + beef seasoned with juniper. People in Wielkopolska prize *metka* – a raw (cold-smoked) and spreadable sausage-meat, as well as *bułczanka*, a *zymlok*-like product made from pigs' heads and livers. Various cooked hams are ever popular, as are delicacies like *polędwica* – pork fillet smoked raw – and *kabanos* – a thin, dried sausage made from best cuts.

Cooked meat served cold or in jelly

Cold cooked pork, beef or poultry are often served at suppertime. Once popular, but now only rarely eaten, półgeski are breasts of goose left in salt in oak for a week, before being sprinkled with bran and cold-smoked for several days. Various kinds of meat or fish in jelly are also served at an evening meal – perhaps pigs' trotters, poultry, tongue, pike, tench or carp.

Pickles and preserves

Exquisite additions to meats served cold are the wide range of sweet or sour pickles, as well as vegetable or fruit preserves. Supreme examples are vinegar-pickled versions of different wild fungi picked in the forest, above all boletus and lactarius mushrooms, chanterelles and certain kinds of agaric. The lactarius mushrooms are also served soured, with salt and spices. This method is often nicknamed "under stone", since the fungi were once placed in a stone basin, and covered with a board with a heavy stone on the top. Cucumbers are really popular, be they larger ones in vinegar, smaller gherkins, or cucumbers "soured" through part-fermentation in water with herbs and spices. Red peppers also get pickled, as do green tomatoes and vegetable salads. Sweeter items in turn involve plums, pears, cherries or grapes. The taste of cold or hot meats may also be set off by a sweet apple sauce or the various preserves made with rowan berries, cranberries or cowberries, often augmented by pear or apple. Preserves, above all of plum and apple, are also served at suppertime.

Polish steak tartare

Mazowsze

300 g beef sirloin/tenderloin,
1 tablespoon oil,
1 tablespoon mustard,
2 egg-yolks,
1 pickled cucumber,
6 small pickled boletus mushrooms,
2 onions,
several leaves of lettuce,
salt and pepper

Clean the meat of membranes and sinew, before mincing moderately finely and adding the oil, mustard, salt and pepper, and mixing well. Divide into two portions, laying each out on a dish on lettuce leaves. Make a well in each pile of meat, carefully pouring an egg-yolk into each. Dice the onion, wild mushrooms and cucumber and lay out around the meat, before seasoning with salt and pepper. Also sprinkle the yolks with pepper. Serve soon after preparation, with bread and butter.

Smoked goose

1 kg breast meat of goose
with skin,
60 g salt,
1 g saltpetre,
1 teaspoon sugar,
2 cups water,
several peppercorns,
allspice,
several juniper berries,
1 bayleaf

Rub the meat over with half of the herbs (having first ground them up and mixed with salt). Boil the remainder of the herbs in 2 cups of water. Cool this marinade before pouring it over the meat laid in an earthenware vessel that has first been steam sterilised, then cover over with a weighted plate so that the meat is fully submerged in the marinade. Leave for two days, before turning the meat over and continuing with the marinading for another 10 days. Check regularly for any frothing of the liquid (should this occur, new marinade will need to be prepared). Then remove the meat, rinse and dry, fold double and sew together with cotton thread. The meat may also be placed in a string bag. The goose is now smoked in a not-too-hot smoke and set aside for 2-3 weeks. At this point it is ready for eating. If not smoked, the goose removed from the marinade may be cooked until tender in water with herbs, before being left to cool in the stock, removed, laid out and squeezed between two boards in a cool place. In either case, the goose is sliced like ham, being served for example with cowberry sauce or fruit pickles.

Eel in the jar

Warmia-Mazury

3 medium-sized smoked eels,
3 fish heads,
1 carrot,
2-3 onions,
1 parsley root,
1 celeriac,
several peppercorns,
allspice,
1 bayleaf

Skin the eels and slice them into pieces around 7 cm long, before putting these into jars. Into each jar drop several peppercorns, the allspice, a bayleaf and several rings of blanched onions. In salted water boil up a stock made from the fish-heads and vegetables. Drain off, pouring the stock over the chunks of eel in the jars before pasteurising for about 40 minutes. Store in a dark, cool place.

Tench á la tripe

Pomerania

fresh tench,
fish stock,
1 carrot,
1 parsley root,
1 celeriac,
1 onion,
parsley,
flour,
salt and pepper,
nutmeg,
ginger,
maggi spice,
2 tablespoons butter,
1 litre water

Gut the fish, also removing the head and fins, fillet, cutting into thin slices. Prepare stock from the fish head. Peel the vegetables, slice, fry lightly in butter and cook in the fish stock. Near the end of the cooking, add the cut-up tench and cook on for several minutes. Prepare a thickener from fried flour and butter, add to the fish stew, along with salt and pepper, the ginger, the nutmeg (grated) and a teaspoonful of the *maggi*. Boil up once again and sprinkle with parsley.

Pork knuckle in beer

Wielkopolska

1½ kg pork knuckle,
2 leeks,
1 celeriac,
3 parsley roots,
5 carrots,
1 large pale ale,
1 small cup brandy,
100 g lard,
1 bayleaf,
allspice,
cumin seeds,
black pepper,
salt

For the curing:
1 litre water,
50 g coarse salt,
50 g curing salt
(salt with a small amount
of sodium nitrite),
1 tablespoon sugar,
garlic,
marjoram,
allspice

Place the pork knuckle in an earthenware basin and pour in the curing liquid, leaving to steep for 7 days. Then remove, rinse, sprinkle with the spices and fry lightly in the heated fat. Dice the vegetables coarsely, add to the knuckle and – at the end of the frying – pour on a small amount of water and simmer on until the vegetables soften. Pour in the beer and cognac slowly and simmer on for a further 20 minutes or so. Serve with cooked sauerkraut and boiled potatoes.

Rolled streaky bacon in herbs

Podlasie

1 kg raw streaky bacon
in thin slices,
250 g smoked streaky bacon,
tablespoon mustard,
2 cloves garlic,
½ teaspoon marjoram,
½ teaspoon thyme,
½ teaspoon tarragon,
salt and pepper

Rub the herbs and spices and crushed garlic into the surface of the raw bacon. Cover and leave in a cool place for several hours. Then lay out the bacon — meat upwards — and cover with the slices of smoked streaky bacon, before spreading with mustard, rolling up and tying with cotton. Place in a thick-bottomed baking tin and put into a well-heated oven. Bake for about 50 minutes at 190ºC. Lower the temperature when the meat begins to brown. When it has cooled, slice the bacon thinly, laying it out on a serving dish and garnishing with pickled plums and pears.

Pig's trotters in jelly

Podkarpacie

1 kg pig's trotters,
1½ litres water,
 stock-vegetables,
salt,
pepper,
2 cloves garlic

Carefully clean and wash the trotters, before sawing into smaller pieces. Put into water and cook on a low heat for around 1 hour. Add the stock-vegetables and cook on, until the meat parts from the bones. Remove the meat from the bones and cut into small pieces, before returning to the liquid and seasoning with salt, pepper and crushed garlic. Pour the jelly mixture into separate small dishes or 1 large bowl, adding thin slices of the cooked carrot. Place in the fridge until fully set.

Polish vegetable salad

Mazowsze

5 medium-sized potatoes,
1 medium-sized carrot,
1 parsley root,
1 celeriac,
1 large onion,
1 large tart apple,
2 medium-sized soured cucumbers,
1 tin green peas,
6 pickled mushrooms caps,
6 plums pickled in sweet sauce,
10 tablespoons
salad mayonnaise

Boil the potatoes in their skins, then leave to cool and peel. Cook the carrot, parsley and celeriac. Dice the potato and vegetables, adding finely-chopped onion, apple, cucumber and the pickles. Add peas and mix thoroughly, adding salt, pepper and sugar to taste. Add the mayonnaise and mix in well.

Cabbage with boletus mushrooms

Świętokrzyskie region

1 kg sauerkraut,
1 jar (0,33 l) pasteurised boletus
mushrooms or 300 g frozen,
1 cup great white beans,
2 onions,
4 tablespoons linseed oil,
1 bayleaf,
100 g destoned prunes,
several peppercorns,
half a teaspoon marjoram,
salt

Soak the beans overnight in pre-boiled water before cooking in the same water with salt and marjoram added. Cut up the cabbage,
place in a pan, and pour on 1 cup of water, adding peppercorns and the bayleaf. Boil so as to steam off the water, then add 2 tablespoonfuls
of the oil. Cut the pasteurised mushrooms into medium-sized chunks (if frozen then first boil for 2-3 minutes in salted water).
Add the mushrooms to the cabbage, along with the onion fried on the remainder of the oil. Cook for several minutes,
then add in the cooked beans, salt to taste and simmer for a short further time.

Pierogi with cabbage and mushrooms

Christmas Eve Supper

Lublin region

For the *pierogi*:
450 g flour,
2 eggs,
2 tablespoons oil,
warm water

For the stuffing:
100 g dried wild mushrooms
(boletuses are best),
1 onion
40 g butter,
1 tablespoon dried breadcrumbs,
salt,
pepper,
pork fat for greasing

Sieve flour on a board, adding 1 egg to it, the oil and the same amount of hot water, ensuring that the resultant dough does not become too stiff. Knead very thoroughly until there is no sticking to the board. Pour warm water on to the washed mushrooms and leave to soak for several hours, before cooking in the same water, draining, drying and mincing. Cook the cabbage, drain and slice. Chop the onion finely and fry in butter, before adding in the minced mushrooms, cabbage and seasonings and leaving to cool. Cut out circles or squares from the rolled-out dough and stuff, before closing up the pierogi. Cook in a large pan of salty water to which a tablespoonful of oil has been added. Serve hot greased with oil and sprinkled with breadcrumbs fried without fat until brown.

Red beet soup (borscht) with "ears"

Mazowsze

Mixture for the "ears":
200 g flour,
1 egg,
2 tablespoons boiled water,
1 teaspoon oil,
salt

Stuffing for the "ears":
200 g dried wild mushrooms (boiled),
1 medium-sized onion,
1 tablespoon butter,
2 tablespoons parsley,
1 tablespoon breadcrumbs,
1 egg,
salt and pepper

For the soup:
500 g beets,
1 litre water,
2 onions,
20 g dried wild mushrooms,
salt,
sugar,
1 bayleaf,
3 cups soured beetroot juice

"Ears": Knead the dough, set aside, and then cut the onion finely and fry in butter until clear. Dry the mushrooms, chop finely and mix in the onion and fry gently. Leave to cool, add the chopped parsley, dried breadcrumbs, salt and pepper to taste, beat the eggs and rub in. Roll the resultant dough out on a floured board, then cut into small squares which are stuffed with the filling and sealed into an "envelope" on both sides. Cook in slightly salted water and drain. Serve with the beetroot soup, preferably soon after cooking.
Soup: Wash the wild mushrooms, then soak them before boiling in the same water and drying off. Peel the beets, cutting them into thin rings, before tipping them into the boiling water. Add the herbs and spices and the onion (quartered) and cook for about 3 minutes. Remove from the flame, cover and set aside for several hours. Then, drain off the beetroot stock and add to it the wild mushroom stock and the soured beetroot juice, making up with a small amount of water until there is about 1½ l of beet soup.

Soup with wild mushrooms

Kujawy-Pomerania

Łazanki noodles:
1½ cups flour,
2 eggs,
water,
salt

Soup:
100 g dried wild mushrooms,
2 carrots,
1 parsley root,
1 small celeriac,
1 leek,
1 large onion,
1 bayleaf,
pepper and salt,
2 litres water

Łazanki noodles: Prepare dough as if making pasta, and roll out thinly. Leave to dry then place one layer above the other (coating each with a pinch of flour to prevent from sticking) and cut into rather wide strips. Cut across each strip to give bands about 1½ cm wide, and then cut these once again to create squares. Boil up water and tip the pieces of łazanki dough into it slowly, stirring to prevent sticking. After cooking, drain and rinse with cold water, before laying out on the plate in which the soup is to be served.

Soup: Wash the wild mushrooms well, then soak for several hours in warm pre-boiled water. Boil up a stock with the vegetables, adding salt, pepper and the bayleaf. Add the mushrooms together with the water in which they have been soaking and cook on until soft. Drain off the mushrooms and stock-vegetables, then cut several of the mushrooms into strips and add to the soup.

Carp in jelly

Lower Silesia

1½ kg carp,
1 small carrot,
a piece of celeriac,
2-3 onions,
salt,
1 tablespoon sugar,
¼ teaspoon pepper,
3 level teaspoons gelatine,
1 litre water

Gut the fish, remove the head, eyes and gills and wash well. Slice the stock-vegetables thinly. Cut the rest of the carp into ring slices and lay these out in a flat vessel with the vegetables, before pouring on water and adding sugar and salt. Cook under cover, simmering very gently for around 1½ hours. Towards the end of the cooking period add the pepper, as well as the gelatine suspended in a couple of tablespoons of water. Cool the carp in the original vessel, tightly covered. Serve the fish with a parsley garnish, slices of hard-boiled egg, plus horseradish, mayonnaise or tartar sauce.

3 herrings,
1 carrot,
1 cup wine vinegar,
1 teaspoon sugar,
4 tablespoons oil,
2 red onions,
several peppercorns
and allspice berries,
1 bayleaf

Rinse and clean out the herring, cutting off the head and tailfin, before cutting into slices. Peel the carrot and cut into slices, then boil in a small amount of water with pepper and the herbs. Cool the liquid down, add the vinegar, sugar and oil and mix. Poor the liquid over the herring, cover and refrigerate for several days. Prior to serving, dry off the fish, and present with some of the aforementioned carrot plus slices of red onion.

Łamaniec biscuits with poppyseed mixture

Małopolska

For the pastry:
2 cups flour,
half packet butter,
4 tablespoons sugar,
 egg-yolks,
1 tablespoon soured cream

For the poppyseed mixture:
2 cups poppyseeds,
3 cups milk,
½ cup honey

Grind the flour and butter into a paste, gradually incorporating the sugar, cream and egg-yolks. Knead the mixture, before refrigerating for 1 hour. Then roll out, cut into triangles and bake for around 15 minutes on a tray at 180ºC, until golden. Douse the poppyseeds with hot milk, then simmer on a low flame for around 15 minutes, before draining and passing through a grinder or crushing by hand. Mix in the honey, place in a small bowl and decorate with the *łamaniec* biscuits.

1 cup poppyseeds,
1 cup wheat,
1 cup honey,
1 litre milk,
200 g walnuts,
50 g each of raisins,
dried figs,
prunes and dried apples

Soak wheat in water overnight, then boil in half of the milk and remove. Heat the rest of the milk and add poppyseeds as it comes to the boil. Cook on a low flame before passing through a grinder, or mashing using pestle and mortar. Mix in the wheat, add the honey, the nuts (chopped) and the dried fruit (chopped after first having been seared with boiling water).

Polish ginger cake

Kujawy-Pomerania

750 g flour,
200 g sugar,
300 g honey,
150 g butter,
5 eggs,
2 teaspoons baking soda,
3 tablespoons soured cream,
2 teaspoons gingerbread spices,
1 tablespoon raisins,
1 tablespoon chopped hazelnuts,
1 tablespoon chopped walnuts,
1 tablespoon orange peel,
butter and breadcrumbs
for the baking tray

Heat the honey, sugar and fat until the mix dissolves and then cool down. Sift the flour into a bowl, adding the honey mass gradually, as well as the seasoning and eggs to create an even mixture. This should assume a creamy consistency, so a mixture that is too stiff may have the soured cream or some kefir added to it. Continue mixing until air bubbles appear at the surface, then add the baking soda (first dissolved in a little cold water) and mix on. Add the fruit and nuts (first flour-coated) at the end, then pour the mixture into tins until one-third full and place in an oven pre-heated to 160° C. Bake for about an hour, checking if the cake is cooked through by using a skewer. When ready, remove and leave in the tins to cool before serving.

Lower Silesia

For the dough:
300 g flour,
1/8 cup milk,
2 egg-yolks,
20 g yeast,
150 g sugar,
2 tablespoons butter,
1 pinch salt

For the filling:
300 g poppyseeds,
250 g sugar,
2 tablespoons chopped walnuts,
1/8 cup hot milk,
1 tablespoon honey,
2 tablespoons butter,
3 tablespoons dried breadcrumbs

Sift the flour into a bowl, add the yeast (as premixed with warm milk and a tablespoonful of sugar), salt, butter and egg-yolks. Stir in until an even dough is obtained before putting aside to rise. Boil up the poppyseeds, drain off and grind up mechanically or by hand. Add the butter, honey, sugar and nuts and fry slightly, before pouring in the milk and adding the egg-whites and breadcrumbs, and mixing well. Divide the dough into three parts, form these into rectangular shapes and spread each with the poppyseed mass. Then roll up and place the rolls in a pyramid on a greased and floured baking sheet. Leave to rise then bake the cake arranged in this way in the oven at a temperature of 180°C.

Dried fruit compote

Łódź region

300 g prunes,
200 g dried apples,
5 medium-sized dried pears,
1 lemon,
2 litres water,
1 cup sugar

Wash the fruit and soak the different types separately in clean water for several hours. Then cook each type separately before combining, sweetening, leaving to cool and pouring into a large jug. Peel a lemon, remove the pips, slice and add to the compote before serving.

Tarninówka:
1 kg sloes,
1½ cups sugar,
1 litre good pure vodka (45%)

Smorodinówka:
5 kg blackcurrants,
3 litres rectified spirit (90%),
7 glasses water,
1½ kg sugar

Tarninówka: Transfer washed sloes (picked in late autumn) to a demijohn, add the sugar and the vodka and seal, leaving for 3-4 weeks. Then drain off, bottling the liqueur and laying down for 4-5 weeks.

Smorodinówka: Top and tail the washed currants, and place in a demijohn with the spirit and 4 glasses of water, leaving at room temperature but in darkness for 6 weeks. Then gauze-filter the spirit into a second vessel, combining with a hot syrup made from 3 glasses of water and 1½ kg sugar. Mix, filter into bottles and leave for several months.

List of dishes

List of dishes

Text
Izabella Byszewska
The author would like to acknowledge her debt to participants in the "Nasze Kulinarne Dziedzictwo"
("Our Culinary Heritage") competition for the inspiration they provided as this book was being written

Photography
Christian Parma

Graphic processing and arrangement of dishes
Marta Marciniak

Preparation of dishes
Michał Borzęcki – Head Chef, Maria Restaurant,
Bożena Śliwczyńska – helper

Translation
James Richards

DTP
Wydawnictwo PARMA PRESS
Olga Baranowska, Eliza Dzienio, Katarzyna Sosnowska

Wydawnictwo PARMA®PRESS
05-270 Marki, al. Józefa Piłsudskiego 189 b
+ 48 22/ 781 16 48, 781 16 49, 781 12 31
e-mail: wydawnictwo@parmapress.com.pl
http://www.parmapress.com.pl

ISBN 978-83-7777-062-7

Marki 2011